THE ADVENTURES OF ALEC THE FLYING FOX

LUKE ROWLAND

ILLUSTRATED BY
LAUREN MOUSLEY

Published by Luke Rowland 2016
www.lukerowlandauthor.com

Text copyright © Luke Rowland 2016

Illustrations © Lauren Mousley 2016

The moral right of the author has been asserted.

All rights reserved. No part of this book may be reproduced or transmitted by any persons or entity, including internet search engines or retailers, in any form or by any means, electronic or mechanical, including photocopying (except under the statutory exceptions provisions of the Australian Copyright Act 1968), recording, scanning or by any information storage and retrieval systems without the prior written permission of the author.

National Library of Australia Cataloguing-in-Publication entry has been applied for.

9780995375703 (Ingram Spark)
9780995375710 (mobi)
9780995375727 (ePub)

Custom book production by Captain Honey
www.captainhoney.com.au

5 4 3 2 1 16 17 18 19 20

Story 1
ALEC'S NEW FRIEND
6

☆

Story 2
ALEC'S BIG NIGHT
28

☆

Story 3
ALEC'S AUSSIE CHRISTMAS
48

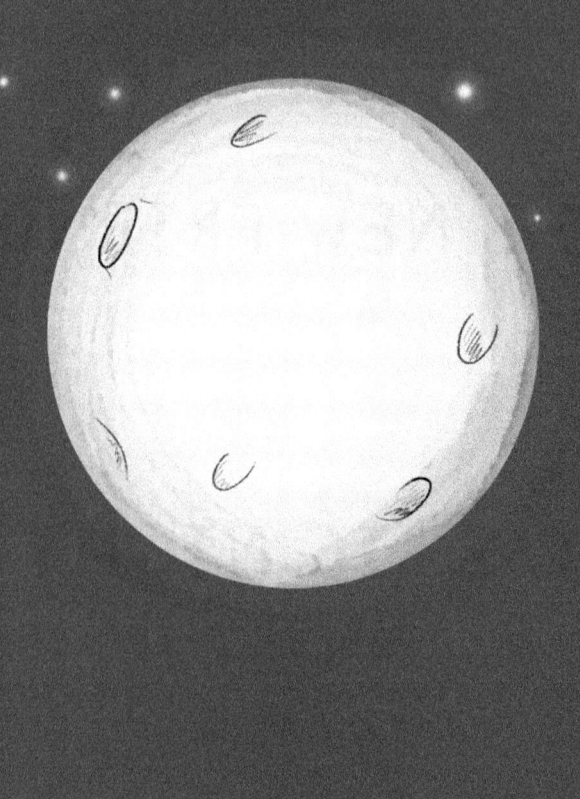

Alec's New Friend

Alec is a young Black Flying-fox pup who lives with his mum and a lot of other flying-foxes in a camp.

A very curious, brave little flying-fox, Alec likes nothing more than to explore with his friends, play games and pretend to go on grand adventures.

His friends names are:

Siana – a Little Red Flying-fox pup (quite small for her age, she could fit in the palm of your hand!)

Big Foot – a Black Flying-fox pup (with very big feet).

The little flying-foxes play games together, like Hide and Seek, Guess the Flower, and Tag You're It!

On one particular night, Alec, Siana, and Big Foot were playing Tag You're It!

'Tag You're It!' cried Siana as she flew past Alec, touching his back with her wing. 'That's what you think' cried Alec as he took off from the branch after her.

They flew this way, and that. Siana was very fast, one of the advantages of being small! Alec was gaining on her, but then he spotted Big Foot flying towards them.

He gave up chasing Siana and instead flew past Big Foot. 'Hi Al-', **'Tag You're It!'** shouted Alec. Big Foot laughed and started chasing them both.

They could feel the wind as they whooshed past each other with lightning speed. As dawn broke, the three pups were worn out from playing all night.

Alec said goodbye to Big Foot and Siana and made his way back to his mum, who was waiting for him to return. She was starting to get a little worried, as Alec was normally back by now.

On the way he heard a voice say 'Hey, come down here'. Alec, being a curious fellow, made his way down to the lower branches of a gum tree. There was a Grey-headed Flying-fox pup all by himself.

'My name's Alec. What's yours?', he asked. 'Ironbark', 'I saw you and your friends playing that game before'. 'Yes it's called "Tag You're it"! Would you like to play sometime?' Alec asked excitedly.

'No way!' Ironbark replied. 'I don't play silly children's games. I'm too old and smart for that'. 'You better stay out of my way, you little freak', he growled at Alec.

Ironbark took off from the branch and flew off into the night, leaving Alec feeling hurt and confused. No

one had ever spoken to him like that before.

The next night, Alec was flying to meet Siana and Big Foot. The sky was beautifully clear, the moon looked full and bright.

'Going to play that stupid little game again freaky?' Alec stopped and threw a nervous glance to his right.

Ironbark flew up next to him. Alec was getting angry, he didn't like the way Ironbark was treating him. 'Why do you call me that?' I've never done anything to you'. Alec started to fly away, but Ironbark followed him.

'I don't know why anyone would want to hang out with an ugly little rat like you', Ironbark said, 'but then

again, your friends are freaks too'.
Using his right wing, Ironbark covered
Alec's face so he couldn't see and then
quickly took it away just as Alec was
approaching a branch. CRASH!

Ironbark cruelly laughed at him and
flew away. Alec, sobbing heavily, beat
his wings very hard, and very fast.

He flew right past the camp and into the forest, where he landed on the branch of a massive gum tree. Alec was out of breath and needed to calm down. He did not understand why Ironbark was being so mean to him.

'Pardon me blossom, but what is the matter?', a voice asked. Alec jumped at the sound and looked along the branch toward the trunk. There sat a koala chewing slowly on some gum leaves.

'I didn't mean to disturb you Miss Koala', Alec sniffled. 'Please, call me Tallow', she replied. 'Come closer dear, I don't bite, tell me your name'.
Alec crawled along the branch towards her. 'My name's Alec, I live just up the hill there', he pointed with his wing.

Tallow looked in the direction Alec was pointing. 'Is there something you would like to talk about?' she asked quietly. Alec began sobbing as he said very quickly 'There is a new kid in our camp and he's bigger and better looking than me, and he called me freaky and I don't know why he's being so nasty!'

'Perhaps this young man has trouble making new friends, or maybe something bad happened to him', Tallow said gently. 'Still that's no reason for being mean, no one deserves to be treated like that'.

She wiped a tear away from his cheek. 'I don't know what to do', Alec said helplessly. 'Perhaps you could

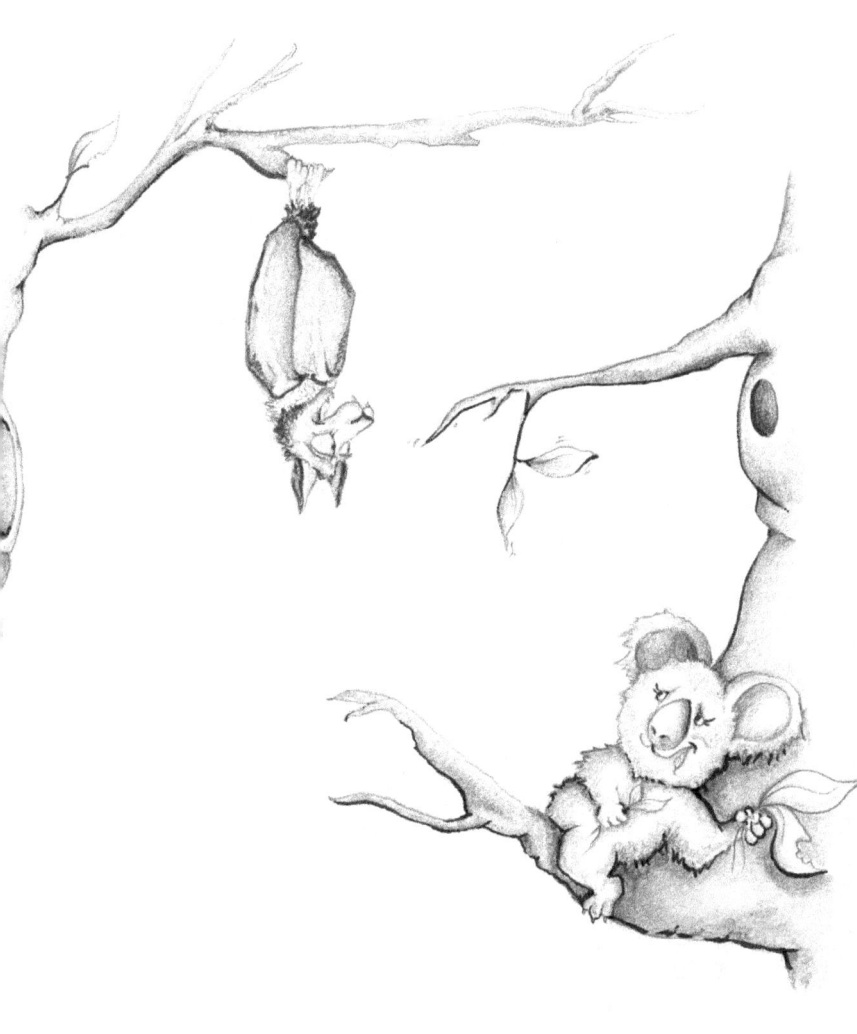

ask him if everything's ok?' Tallow suggested. Alec winced and replied 'But he'll probably just tell me off'.

'Hmmm, maybe invite him when you and your friends are ALL playing together. That way he'll feel included in the group, it's a great way to make new friends', Tallow said. 'That could work', Alec thought to himself.

'I guess I could give it a go', he said. 'Of course you can', Tallow replied. Alec smiled at her, he felt much better. 'Well Tallow, I should be getting back now, thank you for listening to me', Alec said.

'You're most welcome. What a wonderful little flying-fox you are', she chuckled. 'Anytime you want to chat, you know where to find me'.

Alec took off from the branch. 'Goodbye', he cried out, and beating his wings very hard and very fast he headed back to the camp to see his mum.

On the way, Big Foot and Siana came flying up to him. 'Hey Alec, where have you been?' asked Siana. 'Guys, there's something I need to tell you', he replied.

Alec told them about Ironbark and meeting Tallow. The three young flying-foxes then began searching for Ironbark. They looked for him in the treetops, but he wasn't there. They tried looking around the stream, but he wasn't there either.

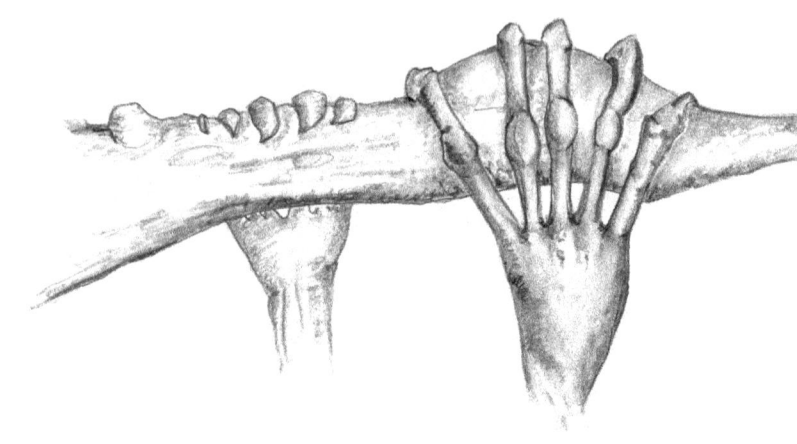

Alec finally spotted him hanging off a branch on a dead tree. 'What do you want?' he rudely asked them. Big Foot spoke first, 'Look, we heard what you've been calling Alec, and it is not acceptable'.

'He's right. Picking on someone for their looks is downright unfair', Siana said as she slapped her wing against

the branch angrily. 'I mean, look at Big Foot and myself. I'm tiny for my age and Big Foot has big feet' She pointed to his feet. They were big!

'It's our differences that make us unique Ironbark', Alec said. Ironbark's heart was beating fast, and tears started forming in his eyes.

'You're right', he said sadly. He looked at Alec, 'I'm sorry for what I called you Alec'. 'My dad and I were all that was left of my camp. We came here after the big yellow monsters knocked down all the trees'.

'That's awful, Ironbark', Siana gasped, I'm sorry to hear that'.

Ironbark held out his right wing towards Alec and asked, 'Alec, can you ever forgive me for what I said'? 'I'm all alone and could really use some friends right now'. Alec nodded at him and held out his right wing, and they locked their thumb hooks together.

'Of course I forgive you', he said. 'Now, how about a game of Tag! You're It'?

Ironbark looked at all three of them and smiled, 'Yes I'd like th- **Tag! You're it**', he touched Alec with his wing and took off.

'Ha!' Alec cried, and beating his wings very hard, and very fast, he chased after Ironbark. The four flying-foxes spent the rest of the night playing games, eating flowers and laughing until they could laugh no more.

Alec was filled with joy. He had helped someone and made a new friend.

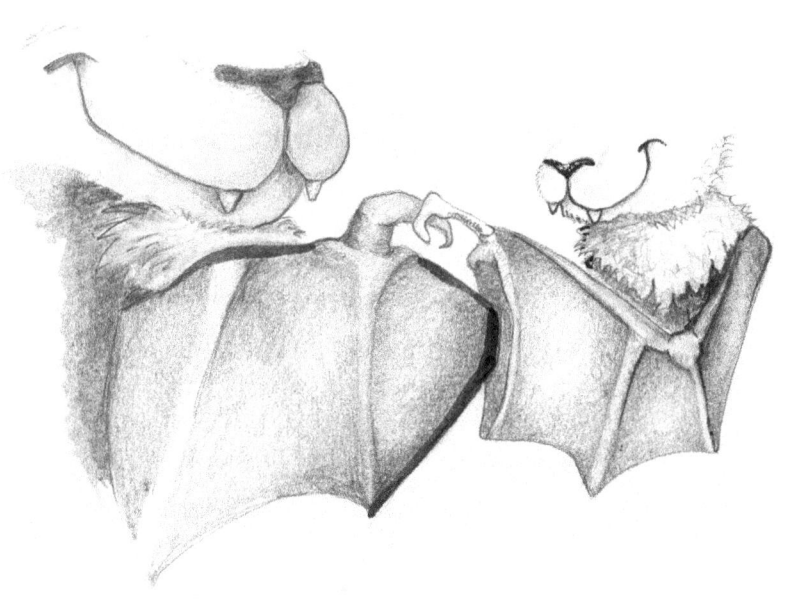

Fun Facts!

- Flying-foxes are a protected species in Australia. However, they face some serious challenges including habitat loss and being shot by farmers for raiding their fruit trees. Also the pups tend to have a high mortality rate, particularly during extreme hot weather periods.

- The females give birth to one pup per year, and the young stays attached to the mother for the first month of its life.

- With their amazing eyesight and fantastic sense of smell, flying-foxes have little trouble searching for their meal at night!

- Big Foot is the name of a Black Flying-fox pup I raised in 2008.
- A small number of flying-foxes carry a couple of viruses, which can be harmful to humans. If you see an injured or dead flying fox on the ground, DO NOT TOUCH IT!! Always tell an adult, and call a wildlife care group who can deal with the animal. Only people who have been vaccinated against these viruses should handle flying-foxes.

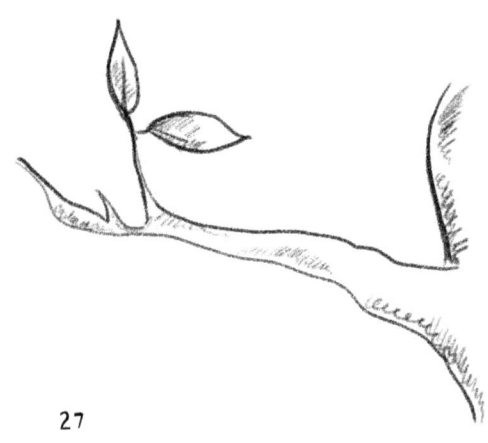

Alec's Big Night

On a very fine starry night, Alec was waiting for his mum to come back with some yummy flowers. He was quite hungry, and was hoping she would bring back his favourite eucalypt flower.

Alec had spent the whole day sleeping. Though it had been a rather hot day, and he did have difficulty getting to sleep at first, a cool breeze eventually lulled him gently to sleep.

Nighttime was Alec's favourite time.

Mrs. Flying-fox went out searching for food all night. She always brought home something delicious to eat. She was always on time, and never late.

Alec didn't like the fact he was small. He wanted to be a big flying-fox and go searching for food like the adults.

He often wondered what exciting adventures he could have far from his home. 'I want to go look for some delicious flowers myself.'

He checked to see if the coast was clear, and then said to himself 'Now's my chance'.

Alec took off from the branch, and beating his wings very hard, and very fast, he left the camp to go on an adventure of his own.

Soaring high into the night sky, Alec felt like a star! 'Now I'm a **big** flying-fox' he said aloud.

It wasn't long before Alec spotted some scrumptious looking flowers on a big gum tree. He landed on a branch with the most flowers.

Alec took a nice big breath, 'ahhhhhhhhh … I love the sweet smell of flowers' he said. **Munch! Munch! Munch!** Alec ate his way up the branch.

Alec was so hungry he ate all the flowers on the branch. Before too long, he was feeling very full.

'Uh I've eaten **SO** much' he said as he looked down at his belly. It was quite round and fat just like a ball.

Alec realized it was getting late. He had to be back at the camp before his mother was, or she'd be very worried about him, and he might get into trouble.

So he took off from the branch, and beating his wings very hard, and very fast, Alec began the long trek home.

As Alec was making his way, he got a strange feeling in his stomach. This isn't the way back, he thought to himself.

He flew this way, and that, but he couldn't remember. Alec began to feel frightened. He was all alone and very small in the big dark sky.

'Why did I leave the camp?' he asked himself. 'Mum and all my friends are going to be wondering where I am'. All I wanted was to be a big flying-fox, he thought.

Alec spotted a dark shape in the tree ahead. He flew towards it and landed a little too noisily on the nearest branch. 'Hey!' a voice said, 'You woke me up!' Alec had accidently disturbed a **very** grumpy Magpie.

'Excuse me Mr. Magpie, but I've lost my way home. Could you help me please?' Alec asked.

'NO!' the Magpie replied, 'I'm trying to sleep, now be on your way'. And the grumpy Magpie turned his head, closed his eyes and promptly fell back to sleep.

'Sorry for disturbing you' Alec said

quietly, and took off again into the night.

Alec saw an owl and her three owlets on a fence. He flew down and asked 'Please help me, I'm lost and need help getting home'. The owl smiled at him, 'Of course dear, you just keep following the bright lights', and she pointed to the street lamps with her wing.

'Oh thank you!' Alec said. 'Goodbye! Good luck!' the owlets cried after him.

He followed the street lamps until he came to the end of the street. **Now** where do I go? he thought.

'You look a little lossssst there', a voice said. Alec looked down, and there was a big carpet python

slithering on the ground.

Alec flew down to meet him, 'Yes I am, I need to get back home before my mum does', he said. '

Well then, keep going that way (he pointed with his tail) until you reach a ssssssstream', the snake advised. 'Oh thank you very much', replied Alec.

He continued on his way until he came to the stream, just as the Snake had said. Ok, this is starting to feel familiar, Alec thought.

Looking down at the stream, Alec realised he was feeling quite thirsty, so he flew to the nearest tree and he had a nice drink by licking the dew off the leaves. Feeling refreshed, he continued his journey home.

Alec heard a voice cry out, 'Hello there!'

He flew to the entrance of a small hollow. 'You look awfully young to be out by yourself tonight little man', the voice said.

'Where are you?' Alec asked. 'I can't see you'.

'Right here', the voice replied. 'OH!' Alec cried out. He saw a piece of bark moving towards him. But Alec quickly realised that it was, in fact, a Gecko.

'You are very well camouflaged', Alec said. 'Why of course, my camouflage helps keep me safe from big animals', the Gecko replied. 'That is so cool! Alec was quite impressed.

'Could you help me?' Alec asked.

'I'm lost and need to get home'.

'What is all this commotion?' a gruff voice asked from inside the hollow. 'Did I hear correctly someone is lost?'

An elderly Greater Glider poked his head out of the hollow. 'Yes indeed old sport, this young man is lost', the Gecko replied. Alec was feeling sad, and he started to cry.

He wanted to be home with his mum and all his friends.

'What are those tears for?' she asked.

'Yes, don't despair, you're nearly there', added the Glider.

But dawn was fast approaching and Mrs. Flying-fox had just arrived back at the camp!

'Alec, Alec where are you?', she called out. 'I've bought you back your favourite flowers'.

When Alec didn't answer, she began to get worried. She flew this way, and that, looking for Alec but he was nowhere to be found.

Pointing with her stubby toe the Gecko said to Alec, 'do you see that hill up there? 'Yes I do', he replied.

'I believe beyond that hill is where your camp lies'. 'Yes yes that way!' the Glider said excitedly.

Alec's heart began pounding with joy, for he knew they were right. 'Oh how silly I was not to pay attention to where I was going', Alec said.

'Better be off then, the sun will be rising very soon', said the Gecko. Alec started flying towards the hill. 'Thank you both **SO** much!', he called over his shoulder. 'Quite alright, and don't wander off so far next time!' the Glider shouted after him.

Alec beat his wings very fast, and very hard. He was almost home. As he flew over the hill, he saw big flying-foxes heading towards a clump of big trees. 'Oh I made it'! he cried with great relief.

Alec spotted his mum, and beating his wings harder and faster than ever before, he flew … straight into her! Oops. He gave her a big hug. 'Alec where have you been?' she asked him. 'I was very worried'.

'I'm sorry mum, I just wanted to be a big flying-fox', Alec replied. She smiled at him and said 'Sweetheart, you'll be big soon enough, just enjoy being you for now'. But Alec, you must never leave the safety of the camp again, promise me?'

'I promise', Alec said. As he looked out at the horizon, the sun was just coming up.

'Mum,' Alec said 'I've got quite a story to tell you, I've had a very big night!'

Fun Facts!

- Flying-foxes live in large campsites. As many as 200,000 individuals can be found in a camp.

- Baby flying-foxes are called pups, just like dogs!

- Flying foxes eat the nectar from the flowers of eucalyptus and melaleuca tree species. They spread the pollen from these flowers over great distances to the stigma of other flowers. This is called cross-pollination and some eucalypt species rely on flying-foxes to do this.

- Seed dispersal is when a flying-fox consumes the flesh of the fruit from the tree, then spits out the seed, or the seed passes through their gut quite quickly and is dispersed a great distance away from the host tree. Both of these methods encourage new trees to grow, so flying-foxes play a very important role in our environment. They're nature's gardeners!

- Flying foxes are the only mammals capable of continuous flight. They can cover up to 50kms a night!

- Hollows in old trees provide shelter and a home for many different types of animals, so it's very important to keep these old trees intact.

- Some people think flying-foxes are dirty, smelly creatures. This is not true. They are very hygienic animals, using their tongues to constantly clean their fur and wing membranes.

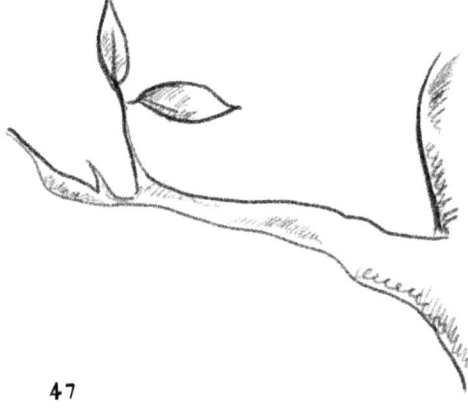

Alec's Aussie Christmas

Alec's favourite time of year is Christmas. This is when flying-foxes from other camps come together to celebrate with friends and family and feast on the yummy blossoming flowers.

For Alec and his mum, it was tradition to fly out into the forest on Christmas Eve to spread some Christmas cheer to the wildlife of Australia.

This year Alec's friends, Siana, Big Foot, and Ironbark, were joining him. As they were getting ready to leave, Mrs. Flying-fox asked them

'So, what do you guys like about Christmas?'

'I like the pretty flowers that are blooming', said Siana.

'I like catching up with my little cousins', said Big Foot.

Ironbark thought for a moment before replying, 'I'm just grateful to be spending Christmas with my new family'. She smiled at him and said 'I'm glad to hear that'.

'Ok, are you four ready?' Mrs. Flying-fox asked.

'YES!' they all replied in unison.

'Then let's go'.

They took off from the branch, and beating their wings very hard, and very fast, left the camp.

It was quite a warm night on this particular Christmas Eve. The moon was full and bright, like a headlight. The crickets were chirping and the frogs croaking.

As Alec, his mum and friends flew past a massive gum tree, they heard a voice above them cry out 'Merry Christmas!' They flew to the top branches to find Tallow the Koala munching on some leaves.

'Merry Christmas', they all replied.

'What do you like most about Christmas Tallow?'

asked Alec. 'I like the warm weather and visits from you Alec', she smiled at him. 'I mean all of you' she added quickly.

Alec and his friends laughed. 'Well we must keep going. Lots of visiting to do', said Siana. 'Of course! Don't let me keep you'. The five flying-foxes took off again into the night. 'Merry Christmas', they called again behind them.

The five flying-foxes visited many different and fascinating animals. Some animals had fur and claws, some had scales and could swim under water, and others had feathers and soared high in the sky.

Mrs. Flying-fox led them down to a nice cool stream, where they could hear the frogs croaking to one another.

Ironbark spotted two Green Tree Frogs sitting on a lily pad.

'*Ribbit Ribbit* Merry Christmas', the frogs said together.

'Merry Christmas to you. Say, are you two twins?' asked Siana.

'Yes indeed *Ribbit Ribbit* we are' they replied together. The twins were brother and sister, and looked identical in every way. Down to the last freckle on their cheeks.

'What do you like most about Christmas?' asked Alec.

'See that beautiful *Ribbit Ribbit* red flower there? The frogs pointed to a flower on a lily pily. 'That flower *Ribbit Ribbit* only grows this time of year *Ribbit*.'

He was right, there were lots of pretty blooming flowers along the banks of the stream. 'That is lovely. Come children we must keep going' said Mrs. Flying-fox. 'Have a great Christmas you two' beamed Alec.

They all kept flying along the stream. After a while, Mrs. Flying-fox and the four friends flew away from the stream and up amongst the trees. Alec spotted something gliding from one tree to another. It was very fast. So fast, Alec had trouble seeing where it went.

Then he felt something brush across his head as it slipped into the tree canopy. Out of the corner of his eye, he caught sight of a Squirrel Glider. Alec broke away from his friends and followed the Glider to a broken tree branch.

'Sorry for bumping you old sport' he said.

'Quite alright' replied Alec.

The others caught up to him and Siana said to the Glider 'Merry Christmas'. 'Well that is nice, and same to all of you' he replied.

'What do you like most about Christmas?' asked Ironbark.

'The green leaves that grow on the gum trees, they are simply delicious!' he said excitedly. 'Here, try some', he pointed to a branch that had lovely soft looking leaves.

The five flying-foxes crawled to the end of the branch. Using his left thumb hook, Alec bought the leaves to his mouth and was the first to try. He took a big bite. Munch! Munch! Munch!

He screwed up his face like he'd just eaten a lemon, and quickly spat them out. The others tried not to laugh as Alec shook his head at them. 'Well, what do you think?' asked the Glider. 'I don't know how Tallow eats this stuff all the time' Alec said to everyone.

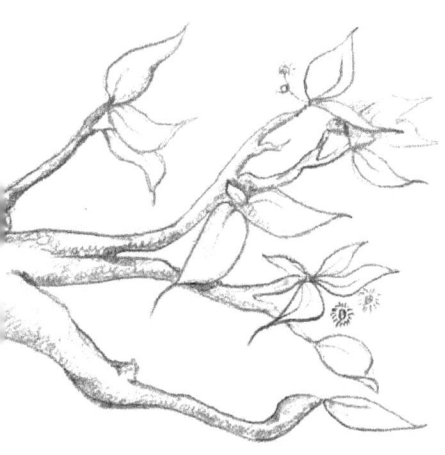

Mrs. Flying-fox looked out at the horizon, where the first light of dawn was emerging 'We had best be off now, Merry Christmas to you' she said. 'Have a great Christmas everyone' cried Glider as the group took off from the branch.

The last stop they made was to Mr. Spike, an Echidna, who lived not far from the camp. At first they mistook him for a soccer ball, but he was just all curled up!

'Merry Christmas to you' Alec said as he and his friends landed on the lowest branch of a small tree. Mr. Spike slowly uncurled and looked up at the group. 'Merry Christmas to you all' he replied.

'What do you like most about Christmas?' asked Alec.

'My favourite type of termites are around this time of year. I lick them up as they scurry into their mound. There are plenty of ants too!'

The sunlight was starting to touch the tips of the trees. It was Christmas Day!

Alec, his mum and friends wished Mr. Spike a Merry Christmas again before making the short flight back to the camp. When they arrived, Siana and Big Foot said Merry Christmas to the others and then went to celebrate with their families.

Alec, Ironbark and Mrs. Flying-fox flew to their branch, saying Merry Christmas to friends and neighbours along the way. A surprise was waiting for Alec and Ironbark when they landed.

'Look Ironbark, she's collected our favourite flowers!' Thank you mum.' He gave her a big hug. 'Merry Christmas Alec, Merry Christmas Ironbark' she said. 'This is the best Christmas ever!' cried Alec. 'Thank you Mrs. Flying-fox' said Ironbark.

It was a fine hot day that day. There was much celebration to be had, on that hill with the big clump of trees. The hill that was Alec's home.

The End

Fun Facts!

- There are four different types of flying-fox in Australia. The Grey-headed Flying-fox, the Black Flying-fox, the Little Red Flying-fox and the Spectacled Flying-fox.

- One of the ways we can help the flying-fox is by planting native trees. Visit your local nursery for more information and try to find a list of species that grow in your area.

- Large, predatory animals such as snakes, owls and sea eagles prey on young, sick or elderly flying-foxes. This helps to keep the population healthy.

- Flying-fox camps are often found near rivers or streams, which provide them with fresh water to drink. A cool way these animals drink is by flying over the water's surface and skimming their bellies into the water. Back in the trees they then lick the water off their bellies!

- In the wild flying-foxes live up to the age of 12. Captive individuals have been known to live over 20 years.

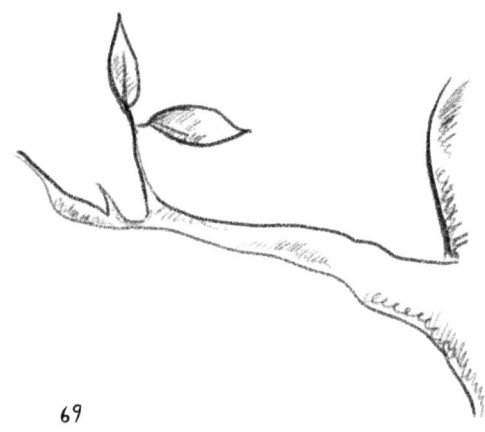

www.ingramcontent.com/pod-product-compliance
Ingram Content Group UK Ltd.
Pitfield, Milton Keynes, MK11 3LW, UK
UKHW021257180426
11947UKWH00015B/886